CW01589967

The Sisyphus Dog

THE SISYPHUS DOG

STEPHEN BOYCE

To Gomota
with warmest thanks
for the invitation.
Stephen
Nov. 2019.

worple press

First published in 2014 by
Worple Press
Achill Sound, 2b Dry Hill Road
Tonbridge
Kent TN9 1LX.
www.worplepress.co.uk

Cover Image: Machine embroidery *The Sisyphus Dog* (detail) 2013 by Alice Kettle (www.alicekettle.com)
Cover photography: Joe Low (www.joelow.com)

Printed by imprintdigital
Upton Pyne, Exeter
www.imprintdigital.net

Typeset by narrator
www.narrator.me.uk
enquiries@narrator.me.uk

ISBN: 978-1-905208-23-4

Acknowledgements

Thanks are due to the editors of the following publications in which some of these poems first appeared – *14 magazine; Antiphon; Ariadne's Thread; Guided by Surprise; Ink, Sweat & Tears; Lyrical Beats; South; The Ofi Press; Visible Breath; Wivenhoe Poetry 2011; Ver Prize Anthology 2012; Poetry & All That Jazz 2012.*

Vows, Late Summer and *Telescope* won third prize in the Plough Prize open and short poem categories respectively in 2009. *Harvesting Tea* won third prize in the Ware Poets Competition 2012.

The Palette was commissioned by Hampshire County Council to accompany the exhibition 'Land, Sea, Sky' in 2011.

Chai Wallah was nominated for the Forward Prize 2012 Best Single Poem.

I am grateful to Alison Hill, Joan McGavin, Keiren Phelan, Simon Richey and Maggie Sawkins for their advice. Special thanks to Alice Kettle for her insight and skill and to Peter Carpenter for enthusiasm and rigour.

For my boon companions
Rob, Harry and Duncan

'Every memory we have is finally of ourselves. If the memory of an experience is flawed, there is a rift in the continuity of self. There is less of us with each depleted memory.'

Don DeLillo (*That Day in Rome – Movies and Memory*, The New Yorker, 2003)

'There is for all of us a twilit zone of time, stretching back for a generation or two before we were born, which never quite belongs to the rest of history. Our elders have talked their memories into our memories until we come to possess some sense of a continuity exceeding and traversing our own individual being.'

Conor Cruse O'Brien (*Maria Cross: imaginative patterns in a group of modern Catholic writers*, Academy Guild Press 1963)

'There are some things one remembers even though they may never have happened.'

Harold Pinter (*Old Times*)

Contents

Counting the Pips

Threads

She pulls the woollen sock up over her wrist,
the hole in its heel like a tonsured head,
where the wooden mushroom sits in her fist.

With the thimble on, she takes up needle and thread
and is lost in the cheerless rhythm of sewing,
she sees only the pattern his journeys make
as he weaves along country lanes, going
battery to battery by truck or bike:
from dugouts in Enfield to searchlights on the coast,
ack-ack emplacements around Cardiff Bay,
or a farm at Tilbury with its concrete gunpost.

And as she tightens each stitch she straightens his way,
drawing him safely home from the docks
to the room where she darns to the ticking of clocks.

Chai Wallah

The siren wails its nightly complaint
as she steps down into the Anderson shelter,
the baby asleep on her shoulder
and a small wooden box wedged
in the crook of her arm.

Moonlight picks out the pencilled words:
"Capt. M.W. Boyce, gift parcel.
Pure Darjeeling. 1lb nett., 3s paid."

After the war he'll use that box
to store old nails and carpet tacks.
And every morning of their long marriage
he will bring her tea in bed – Orange
Pekoe from Ceylon, first flush Assam,
Darjeeling from Namring, Puttabong,
estates he'll visit when the battery stands down,
homes his men will, for a time, return to.

He'll warm the pot, add leaves, stir
and steep as he inhales the malty steam.
This will be the moment, whatever age he is,
when he'll consider the distance
between a box of nails and a box of tea,
between an infusion of leaves
and the small vibrations of a monsoon,
softly brewing.

Home from the War

A wooden camel train from the souks of Cairo,
smooth, unpolished, weightless as sirocco wind,
the red string that once tethered their necks now broken,
blood trail on the mantlepiece where two elephants,
half-tusked, bookend maps and leather-bound heirlooms
just as the train bookends his days, the couplings
and their carriages jolting like the lurch of camels.

Harvesting Tea

The *sahib* is being shown around the tea garden,
face red as a pomegranate flower, brow sparkling
with sweat.

The women must smile, dazzle like their saris.
They raise their heads, straighten, lift the baskets,
cast in

fresh shoots of tea plant in flickering palmfuls,
second flush prayers – invocations that will startle
his tongue

with visions of Chittagong, and longing ever after
for the contoured hills of Udalia gardens.
Years later,

picnicking on his monsoon cape in the margin
of a field, the boys squabbling over his army
telescope,

his wife stoically unwrapping warm tomato
sandwiches, he retreats to the boot of the car
to pour tea

from a thermos, and is momentarily disarmed
by the sound of women keening, by the scars
on their fingers.

Telescope

My father had a brass field telescope
its shaft wrapped in black webbing
and a tiny eyelid at the viewing end
that slid aside revealing ships at sea,
swallows in flight, cathedral spires,
at night the moon and yellow stars.
A cap with a milled edge snapped
over the larger lens so that, folded,
the tube contained the whole round
world, and all the life I ever wanted.

A Certain Slant

Every shared experience – and many that weren't shared,
that were peculiar to one or other of them –
became a tale re-told,
and in the re-telling further distilled
into story, memory of story,
recollection of memory of story, becoming
a new thing which might be called 'the performance'.

So that the experience itself seemed to reside elsewhere,
in certain expressions on their faces
found in the many photographs,
or in the accumulation of those expressions;
in certain objects, redolent and shared – to some extent shared,
though neither knew what the other truly felt
about them – objects such as a political newspaper,
a basket, a seed pod, an unused stamp; but, in time,
even these would take on a reputation,
a certain slant on the story they told.

Letters, on the other hand, written in the heat
of the moment, raw, unfiltered,
unrehearsed, carried something more immediate,
captured something – as in the blinking of a lens –
that was what it was, that could not be changed,
only read by the eyes that read it
at the time it was read,
that came closer the more it was read.

And the greater the distance in time,
the more faded the writing,
the more vivid was the experience
and the nearer the truth of its telling.

Correspondence

Take a small parcel of airmail letters
the colour of fading wood anemones,
their paper more translucent by the decade
like the pale skin on the back of his hand,
the inky script a tattoo or twisted vein.

Unnoticed by the censor's narrowed eye,
these pinpricks of distilled desire
seem to lie just beneath the surface,
the worked lines of his longing, indelible
instructions in the art of endurance.

Kernels

Plums simmering in the pan,
we'd take a hammer to the stones,
prise out the kernel,
stir it in the brew for flavour.

Shrivelled seeds we discarded
with the broken shell,
the trace of cyanide rancid
in our mouths till we licked the spoon.

Those nights when a child wakes,
febrile, fearful, withering
in her cracked hull, comfort her –
sweeten her tongue with plums.

Washing Day

When Gillian stuck her fingers
in her mother's new electric wringer
it was as if all the lights came on at once,
with the kettle and toaster and washing tub,
and all the Atlas lightbulbs exploded as one.
The room was suddenly flooded with screams.

Much later, after the rollers were gently released,
and Gillian's hand had been seen by a nurse,
her mother, in her apron, carried me across
the street high on her shoulder, the tears
drying on my cheek, and my heart
full as a billowing sheet.

Cuban Heels

He had dandy feet in those days,
wore white leather loafers with shiny soles
or cord sneakers with rope for laces,
brothel creepers, espadrilles in summer
– *huarache sandals too* – and tapered
brogues, tan polished, for best.
Dance nights he wore green cuban-heeled
boots bought in Carnaby Street,
with coarse tartan trews, pink corduroys
or bell bottoms flailing heel-and-toe
heel-and-toe, in the centre of the floor,
alive, alive to the shuck and jive,
the click and stamp, the heel spin.

Nowadays his shoes take an age
to soften to the foot's mould,
the awkward flex of his ankle,
weight of bone and angle of instep,
the way his toes have splayed over the years.
He bothers about the tread and scuff
of daily wear. So he settles for sensible shoes
with thick soles and strong leather uppers
– mid-brown – shoes with names
like Windsor, Embassy, Suffolk,
comfortable and roomy,
so he can stand, stiff but steady
and with no sense of sway.

When the mood takes him he is still known
to skip down the road like a child.

Change of Address

Among the legacy of cards and letters,
Christmas lists and children's drawings,
my mother kept her old address books,
the chronicle of our migrations.

Here thick black lines denote the weaving
of our lives, threads sometimes broken,
sometimes trailing; the whereabouts
of sons who move from home to home
scored through without apparent doubt
or hesitation – lives clearly on the up;
or cousins, marrying and changing name –
some more than once – only half obliterated.

And here, crossed out, the names of friends,
some of whom we know from photographs,
some we cannot place, an older generation
dying in their ones and twos – a horizontal
line through "Babs" or "George" or "Bunny",
whichever one was next.

Now in someone else's well-thumbed
leather-bound address book a line
is drawn through mother's name,
together with the ampersand of sixty years
or more that bound her to my father.

The Gift

You were a heaving snowdrift driven hard
against the stiffening hedgerow of my chest.

I tried to melt you in my brittle arms
but the gale rammed your cold white mass tight

between my ribs. My bones ached. The wind dropped.
You stopped wheezing, became translucent

in the calm. It was only when the last
crystals softened on buds and thorns, only then

I knew the precious gift you'd left me.

Mother Explains the Value of School

My son is holding between thumb and index,
index and thumb, the four corners of a postcard.
Six euros apiece *on the net*, or so he tells me,
these sepia photos of old Bruges:
the Belfry – I recall its metallic peal,
all cogs and wheels; those indolent canals,
and here my convent school peering
over the wall as if on tiptoe.

Notre Dame aux Epines – he splays the cards –
Salle de Gymnastique, Plaine Tennis, Réfectoire.

It's all coming back to me, pinafore dress,
straw hat, serial number, everything, even
the tortoiseshell hairbrush, keepsakes of fine hair,
a heap of hairpins like pine needles in the dust
of the boulevard. My fingers can still feel
the milled edge, the engraved initials on my knife,
fork and spoon – worn but not effaced.
Collectors' items, he says, *worth a bit.*

I have planted a thought. He slips the postcard
back into its envelope. He won't let it fade.

Visitors

The smallest movement startles him:
the clock's hands, a stray hair, petals
falling from chrysanthemums
someone has placed on the table.

He struggles to decipher the code
of finches scratching at the rooftiles,
flitting between chimneys.
                                        Distracted
by the chatter of nurses busy
in the corridor, he flaps and flutters
at my clumsy words as rooks wheel
and caw above leafless trees.

He twitches at the touch of his own hand,
crooked fingers, raised veins, the nails
that glisten.
                    My presence makes him ill
at ease; behind me a jackdaw
has appeared at the window in priest's robes.

I have perched here long enough
listening and waiting.
                              I too take flight.

Ways and Means

It means a lot to me that you still visit
– eyes clouded with that thin film of regret.

No meaning passes between us now, only words
– can't understand what we haven't heard.

These old dears mean well – endlessly going on
about their children and *the hell of being old.*

The nurse is mean sometimes – is spiteful
in her scrubbing, doesn't hear me when I call.

I mean to leave this place one day soon
– under my own steam, of my own volition.

David Niven's Smile

I'm in the food court of a mall
on Boylston Street in Boston
and see my father, taller
than in life and pretending
to be Salvador Dali.

Frail, still genteel, huffing a little,
he chunters as old men do,
absorbed in arranging chairs,
tidying the table
with his scrawny fingers,
as he waits for his companions
to bring food.
                    He doesn't eat,
leans forward to listen,
arms clasped about his chest
as if stopping his bag of bones
from clattering into the crockery;
when he speaks his chin trembles
beneath veined cheeks.

The hair is slick and long,
moustache white now, straggly,
no longer clipped or preened,
eyes hooded, brow cross-hatched
like rotten timber; the hawkish nose,
drooping earlobes elongate
his lined face.
                    Even his smile
is taller – and more like David Niven's.

Sky Writing

Three Spitfires passed over Southampton Water
that day, their neat delta pointing to the clutch
of letters in my fist, the drone of Merlins
as unmistakable as the dry sound
of your voice in the blue ink.

I'd been studying your script all week, that sleek
particular copperplate which had secured
your first job; a practised hand of neat loops
and streamlined strokes, elegant without flourish,
that revealed endeavour and a touch of vanity,
perfect for the ledger in which both sides
are required to balance.

The arrowhead shrank as it banked over Hythe
and the pages slid from my hand, whipped up
in the slipstream and spiralling into the sky,
as I listened to the engine note – strangely
familiar – now fading away.

Counting the Pips

"O Captain! my Captain! rise up and hear the bells..."
Walt Whitman

I have your three pips on the epaulettes
from your tropical battle dress, packed
in the small back drawer of the military chest
among the assortment of cap badges,
brass buttons and flashes that you kept.

Most mornings I squeeze a lemon into a cup,
add honey and hot water and count the pips
– which I carefully remove with a teaspoon –
as I listen to the weather, time signal, news.

And every day I think of you in singlet
and knee-length khaki shorts, sweating it out
beyond the Brahmaputra, tipping toads
out of your boots, swilling chai in the heat,
hoping not to come face to face with a 'Jap',
and writing letters longing to be home
to care for her and the little chap –
the first of another three pips, as it turned out.

Protected Species

Playing hide-and-seek with a slow worm
as I turn the compost heap, I'm thinking:

this love between fathers and sons,
in the end it doesn't go unrequited.

We turn to each other in an unbroken
figure-of-eight not knowing head from tail

as we slither through the undergrowth
discovering ourselves, finding each other.

And we return to the same spot every year,
boon companions among seed-heads and peelings.

A Gift Forever

In memory of Sanjay

We watch them hatch
awkward and ungainly,

eager within their taut skin,
wings straining to unfurl

at their sticky opening.
They falter and surge.

In their precious eyes
is all our yearning.

A moment in their presence
is a gift forever. Look up!

A feather floats in the clear sky,
strength and gentleness entwined.

Vows, Late Summer

for J & S

When the room falls silent I'll sit with you
and remind you how, like bonsai masters,
we planted on rock – *ishi seki* –
anchoring the roots of our slant tree
with its soft cumulus of leaves,
its col of moss and bark.

When darkness comes knocking I'll help you
read the patterns of our love;
how like the spirals of shells,
cones and seed-heads they are:
mathematical and improbable,
beautiful and enduring.

And if we falter I'll take you where
the ladder-maker splits chestnut limbs
and joins the matching halves
with rungs wider at the base
than at the apex, the whole apparatus
flexing as we climb,

and I'll show you how the view from the roof
is always of a garden, its borders
like a summer dress thrown off,
with a gate, open, into the orchard beyond.

Marking the Place

Going South

The Oxo Tower stands out tic-tac-toe
against the table of the night.

I cross the Thames from tapas bar
to Waterloo – last train home,

hollowed steps, roll of honour
and the late night final.

It's all so familiar – going south –
even in the half-light of mid-summer

as we pass Edwardian terraces,
acres of well-bred semis,

what remains of woods and fields
where I learned my own sullen art.

Right now I know how swallows feel
though they cross continents,

my direction finder is hardwired
to this territory, my bloodstream

pulses with positioning data,
I am following the pull and tilt

– and not always for the better.

The Lesson

for Vim

On my back in the pool
as the morning sun sweeps round
from behind the hills
and swallows skim the surface of the water,
I'm staring into the blue.
And it feels like falling.

Like falling upwards,
sudden and vertiginous.

Disentangled from the net
of light that laps around me,
beyond the filmy globs in my eyes,
the wisps of white that float
above the valley slopes,
I am falling.

Falling upwards.
Into the blue, the endless blue.

And I remember asking you
as we sat beneath the wisteria
while your tears were drying
and lizards scurried into the shade:
"When does falling become floating?"

And you said: "You'll know.
If you only let go."

All week the red-backed shrike was in the acacia,
among its ripening purple pods,
urging her fledglings
into their first breathless
and uncertain flight.

Convalescence, St Rémy

Van Gogh was going quietly mad,
as I recall, prowling the vestibule
trying to decide if suicide
was really worth it.

I chose the *Loup de Mer,*
verre de Rosé, tarte fine aux pommes.

He had plucked iris
from the walled garden,
pinned their bruised blooms
to his canvas to release their smell.

You had *Magret de Canard, eau minérale,*
Panacotta à la Vanille de Bourbon.

He had smeared his face with pigment;
the other inmates muttered
at the sad holes
he poked for his eyes.

We were together alone. November,
the vine leaves had turned.

I guess he saw you from the asylum window,
met your gaze and thought better of it,
wrote to his brother for money instead.

Côte Vermeille

No less than the kings of Majorca,
he gave you Collioure as dowry,
Salses, the salt pans and all the coast
of Roussillon; for jewels twinkling nets
of light strung along the hulls of fishing barques,
the watery eyes of intricate forts –
soft pinks and yellows – sardines rippling
the silver sea; for perfumes the scent
of rosemary and fennel clinging
to the hillside among cork trees and vines;
for music the sound of sails as they billow
and snap, the creaking skeleton
of a windmill grinding olives
and, in the evening, the rhythm of sardana,
the tramontane soft against your cheek
as you sat beneath the palms, for,
he reasoned royally, why have the empire
when the promenade alone is princely?

Stones

for Dave Billings

I nearly went arse over tip on the footpath to Lundy Bay
where violets, primrose and spring squill were jostling
in the last of the sun with scurvygrass and speedwell.

I clambered over the boulders, with half an eye on the tide
that sucked and slopped in the hollows, as I looked for pretties
and paperweights – for stones are a comfort in sorrow.

And I turned up granite and quartz, flat skimmers of shale,
limestone smoothed by the ebb and flow, and a slew
of coppery pebbles tumbling down to the foam;

then heaved myself back up the cliff, pockets bulging with rocks,
as a stonechat sang in the tangled gorse and alder swayed
in the wind, while the boats out at sea held their course.

So I bring you nothing but stones and I let these stones
speak for me, that hold their own in the storm, keep faith
with the tide and the land; for we measure in millions
the years they have been here, and the years till they turn to sand.

Stargazing

On the African savannah, say,
or out in Utah, we'd have sky enough
for all the constellations.

Here the hills hem in the sea;
all we can make out are a few wan stars
and the lights across the bay.

If the rain sets in tomorrow
we may yet be glad we saw them.

Reflection

for Simon Richey

I'm thinking of you as I walk up Portland Place,
these tall white buildings elegant, radiant
in the autumn sunshine, the sweeping crescent
a mark of curiosity projecting into this future,
its impulse towards flamboyance restrained
by Ionic subtlety, its cupped hands enfolding
a private garden – a place for contemplation
and unravelling.
                              In Regent's Park four herons,
cool observers of what moves below the water's
cloudy surface, stand sleek-necked, reflective,
beneath an arc of slender paper birches.

Marking the Place

The red route of the A5 lies across
the pages of our life like a silk ribbon
marking the place: Betws,

honeymoon rained off; Wrexham
snowed in, out of work, in love,
you fixing the roof at Llanarmon;

Bridgnorth, changing nappies in a lay-by;
the chiropractor cracking bones
in Shrewsbury. Returning again by

road across these hills – soft rain
in summer, moonlit frost in winter.
The ribbon's faded now, the end frayed.

I ease it gently from the leaves:
Criccieth, November,
stalking dippers on the river.

Tracking

Once when all the snow of the year
had swept down Moel y Plas
filling the lane to Llanarmon hedge-high,
and January had locked the stream in ice
so that nothing, not even a droplet,
was heard, a moorhen
skirted the bank by the house,
its red flash catching the light,
its measured steps laying arrows
in the crisp snow, saying
this is the way I have come.

After the thaw I went out
looking for signs in the scuffed mud
thinking to find a nest in the undergrowth.

I go there still,
waiting for a fresh canvas of snow.

Three Cliffs Bay

The wide sand shelf, shell-specked
and combed by the tide,
will tell the story of our passing
for a short while only.

The walker by the shore,
when pressed,
may recollect dimly
watching us from a distance.

Everything passes:
our trek through the burrows,
the way we parted at the water's edge,
met again where the estuary narrows,
sat among the jetsam;
the stepping stones,
the beckoning and the pause for breath,
the kiss we stole when toe to toe.

The snail and stone circle
will recall nothing,
the egret was preoccupied
and the cliffs had seen it all before.

That's why I hold in my hand
this driftwood,
whale-jawed rememberer
with its tiny all-seeing eye.

Laugharne

Everything is about to turn.

Between the stillness and the flow
two trees look like one;
two stones are simply two.

The robin on a jewelled branch
at the window, head to one side,
listens, just like you.
He, too, measures his day by the tide
easing in and out,
quick slow, quick slow.

Silence exhales softly,
rolls out like a long blank page
where oystercatcher and curlew
make their sudden marks.

The horizon settles snug
in the estuary's broad embrace.
It is all you need for comfort.
That, and the silversmith's cat, unmoved.

The stones cease to glisten as the sun wilts.
Its dying light picks out the trees,
one by one by one.

A heartbeat has come and gone.

Vital Signs

Below the tideline on Killiney beach
you shivered as you told me how
the sisters made you bathe in all weathers.

Your words came and went on the breeze
and there among tar and feathers,
cork and wrack, a bloodstone glistened
like a pulsing heart. In my pocket
its sheen of *sang-de-boeuf* soon faded.

We crossed the country in silence.

Rounding the unfinished jigsaw of Galway
and Mayo, I burnished the pebble
in hope it would help you turn back the years.
By Sligo I knew the rose-in-black-rock
blooms only in brine, the salt glaze of tears.

The Sisyphus Dog

for Roger Norgate

"it's always ourselves we find in the sea'
e. e. cummings

Fully forty minutes we must have leant
on the slipway railing watching him fetch
and carry, fetch and carry, and each time
he opens his mouth and puts down the ball
it comes rolling back as surely as it did
on that bagatelle table we had as kids.

And he hasn't even the wit, poor mutt,
to stick out a foot to stop it, nudge it
back up the slope, as the small distractions
of a dog's life – a trailing rope,
a seal enquiring at the landing stage,
the slap of waves against the harbour wall,
the shadow of a gull, that fish 'n' chippy smell –
each snag his fragile concentration,
till, at the corner of his eye, he spots
the ball on its inevitable descent,
gathering momentum, coming to rest
among the faultless wavelets.

His black brow wrinkles, ears droop
once more as, curious, he trudges
to the water's edge where the tide
delivers up its bobbing catch on which,
anew, he softly clamps his jaw,
then ambles up the ramp, blind
to the damp paw prints, now fading
in the sun. He stops just shy of the top.

Bemused, but not displeased, he looks around
at nothing much, places the ungovernable ball
on the concrete incline – down which again
it rolls with mounting speed – you know the rest.

Fully forty minutes you and I have leant
and watched this unhurried innocent,
patient, oblivious, world weary,
and the day has grown neither longer nor
shorter, no-one has come or gone
but one indefatigable dog – up and down and up
again like an ageing magician condemned
to repeat the same trick over and over.
And what this deadpan canine cannot know
is how our hearts have lifted while he laboured,
how the horizon has grown a little softer,
its boundary has moved a little farther off.

A Boat Named for You

for E & J

1

By King Harry ferry small craft ply the river
for trade and pleasure, and at the tide's edge

a boat that bears your name in stencilled capitals,
a simple rowing boat, carvel built and caulked,

made to last, sleek in length and beam to glide
with ease across the Carrick Roads or up

from Black Rock to Garras Wharf with small loads,
oysters perhaps or sand eels. But today

I see you step over the transom to settle
straight-backed in the stern watching the shore-lap,

waiting for the moment the tide begins to turn.
He eases back, strong on the stroke, feet firm

on the boards, oars rattling in the rowlocks
as the blades shift and the water offers momentum.

2

And where will the little boat take you both?
Stroke for stroke, breath for breath from pontoon

to jetty, among mid stream eddies and
kingfisher reaches? In the shallows, along

the black edge with its necklace of weed,
into reeds where heron and egret

listen all day for the silence of fins?
Through tide pools and wind shadows, up river,

down stream, against the current, with the tide,
from here all the way out to the ocean

where sunset will stipple the surface? And all
in a small boat that bears your name,

with a rower who sees in your eyes
river and river bank beneath wide open skies.

And Snow in the South

I wake before dawn. Is it moonbeams
or icicles prising open the curtains?

The world is too still, its heartbeat
muffled by the night's stiff fall.

We rise to see a snow sky – blue-grey,
intense, massive – now moving on.

The tower and steeple begin to glow
in a pale follow-spot of sunlight.

Below us a snowman wears a crown
of jewelled hogweed and a watery grin.

By mid afternoon there's little to show:
slush-pockets, a goulash of mud and leaves,

air that slavers but doesn't bite
and not even our breath to be seen.

Prospects

I'll have a plain grey roof slate for my headstone,
a flat slab of Cambrian rock
split and dressed by skilled hands using only
the simplest tools; sheer Welsh slate
where dampness recedes like cloud-shadow
scudding over Cadr Idris.

And it should slice cleanly into turfed loam
as if dropped from the sky;
strong against the storm and tilted a little
to shade my head when the sun's at its highest.

Let it measure a countess or more,
be a fitting backdrop
for saxifrage and orchid.

And I want no inscription,
only the chalked names of children
and lovers' heart-framed pledges scratched
on a riven bed of Ffestiniog Blue Grey.

I'll have a headstone of Welsh slate,
set on higher ground.

The rest I will imagine.

The Principle of Uncertainty

Spotting Red

Pointing to *The Haywain*, my father said:
"you see how he uses a dab of red
to lead the eye into the landscape."

Since then I see in every canvas
small touches of scarlet or vermillion –
poppies in a distant field, medal ribbon;

'A' roads in an atlas; shades of brick,
flame or cherry; the sticky *swalk*
of lip-print on the flap of an envelope,

the dot beside a work of art that marks
it sold; the goldfinch with his bloodied cheek,
the frayed handkerchief in which I wrap

small curiosities from the beach for you,
and – once or twice, it's true – the signs of loss,
of life and of life's possibilities.

The Principle of Uncertainty

After Woman Holding her Thumb *by Lucien Freud*

To start with, the sitter isn't sitting. She sprawls
awkwardly across the canvas, naked, an inverted 'L',

pelvis twisted, torso slumped as if she has been tossed,
dead or drunk, on the coverless bed. Not dead;

weary, the weight of her breasts palpable,
one settled across her chest, the other precipitate,

spilling into her armpit. He brings us up close,
wants to rule out uncertainty, deny the viewer's part.

So the left elbow holds the centre of the frame,
the right arm conceals her brow, the fingers of one hand

linking the thumb of the other, closing the circle.
But there's no imagining her story;

he doesn't describe the room, leaves no evidence
of time of day, no indication of provenance or pathology.

He will not let me alter his intention; is telling me
to observe the form, the pallid substance,

the sheen of that skin, arrangement of limbs,
the palms unrecognisable against the sheet.

I see only lumpish flesh taken in abstract;
until I lean my head to one side and discover

the arc of a smile, seraphic, an angel of the highest order.
And I wonder: if I cried out, would she hear me?

Figure with Raised Hands

for Ellie Glover

As for me
I know nothing else but miracles.
Sunshine trickles molten gold
into my upturned palms,
birds fidget in my hat
– nesting has begun.
Their presence is always welcome
and their song a constant joy to me.

I am happy to have them for solace,
the birds and the sun,
I welcome their sociable ways;
their touch heals
and because of them my heart blooms,
its white petals piercing the darkness,
its tenderness making me strong.

Now every sprig of me
is sound of purpose,
I know where I stand
and hold my own,
upright, well rooted
in forest or open field.
And when floodwaters rise
babies will be born in my boughs,
for I know nothing else but miracles.

Burnt Chair

After Made Space *by Kate Theodore*

Restless on my three
wizened
half-cremated legs

I have defeated you,
my slow burn
has cheated you.

I'll not be sat on now,
as sure as eggs;

my blackened twiggy bones
would mark you,

my charred knuckles
turn to dust,
wasted limbs evaporate –

a delicate balance,
uneven, anarchic
taken on trust,

standing
on my own
three pointy feet

still

daring the world
to look at me
as what I was –

a seat, a chair, a throne.

Illuminating the Whitworth

She has the fingers of a pattern cutter,
this museum guide, agile, precise.

She points and beams of light ricochet
off the polished parquet floor, one

for the bad lads, one for the good guys
from Rusholme, Hulme, Moss Side,

one for the Kurdish and Somali women
who parade daily through the park

their wrapped hair, their swathed babies.
We weave from gallery to gallery,

the guide's fingertips shooting sparks
off embroidered mirrorwork, revealing

trails of pomegranates and cockatoos,
cranes – plain and decorated – a web

of yarn fashioned by hand, bindings
for tiny feet, fool's parsley etched into walls.

We are striding through starlight
listening to the language of turbans.

The Palette

After North from Butser Hill *by Annabel Gault*

Here is bronze for the Bronze Age,
the Duke of Burgundy's wings
and rings of lichen;
copper
for the scrubby scarp, the ferrous
underside of a Grizzled Skipper,
Gault clay in the valley bottom;

here's white for the hemmed skirt
of Chalkhill Blue, for the turned
earth and the new lamb;
black
for the immortal yew – gravestone
of ancients, sturdy protector –
for flintstones hacked into axeheads;

now sap green for moss in the combe
and for the three-lobed liverwort;

yellow for the specks of Horseshoe
Vetch on bright southern slopes;

natural grey for distant Froxfield
where Edward Thomas strode,

and indigo for the rising air
at its trembling dew point.

The board seethes with layers
of smeared pigment, elemental,
scutched and scarred, becoming equal
with the ever-churning land.

Riverlight

After River 1 Rilla *by Nick Andrew*

Not so much the scattering of light,
but various concentrations
                    and dispersions of it,
follow the flow like spillage
from jars in an apothecary's window –
cobalt blue,
            carmine,
                        hunter green,
                                    straw gold
all pour through the shallow water.

In the gleaming distance
            – uncertain semblance of a perfect future –
rainbows return,
            surge back through narrow prisms
to meld again into pure white light,
changing speed
            between water, air, and eye.

Are we alive enough for this?
Do we know enough of joy?

A Brush with Renoir

A warm mid-morning at *Les Collettes,*
the young woman strides
through groves of wizened olive trees,
whose pollarded trunks
sprout fresh wands
where the old man has had them pruned.

She has the air of one
comfortable in the presence of poultry,
but pensive, wary.
She glimpses his goat's beard,
flat hat and hollow face
above the balustrade
where he watches her sway
across the gravel, cheeks glowing,
dark hair damp against her neck.

In the studio's north light
she observes the brushes
strapped to his knuckles
like shoots on gnarled bark,
feels each touch of the canvas
as a soft caress on the bloom of her flesh.

The young woman is Hélène Bellon,
model for Jeune Fille Assise, *1908*

Four Portraits

The Dutch Painter

His curls are the colour of articulate shale
in the open cupboard where he shows his work,
a memory of brushstrokes
in the dark background of a Rembrandt.

His eyes glisten with raw pigment,
red and blue like the flame
of a medieval lighthouse
dancing on the choppy midnight sea.

The Vietnamese Psychologist

Comfortable shoes
form a small dark plinth
beneath her linen skirt.

Her smile is straight
and her long plait falls
quite perpendicular to it.

Stillness is everything.

The African Architect

He enters, buttressed and braced,
but still a little wobbly,
a small tremor fading into time-gone-by.

In hands like succulents he holds the camera
as if it were a wounded bird,
still strong enough and determined to fly.

The Cuban Poet

These fingers are eloquent exhibitors
of all kinds of fruit and flowers,
delicate manipulators of leaves and roots.
He points, he palms, he pinches
to conjure scents and textures, juices and infusions.

He holds a cocoa pod, the yellow fruit split,
the slimy seed prolapsed.
He urges us to bite on the bitter nut inside.

The Fox

Smiler Marshall, snow-haired, one-eyed whipper-in,
a hundred and two years old, still hollers
like the Master's horn.

A few rust coloured peg teeth peek out
between his ruddy cheeks,
wiry hairs fur the sagging turkey neck,
curl over his lop-sided collar.

Lost his eye when a whipping wild strand
from a horse's mane
pierced the pupil. Was sacked for taking time off
to have his glass eye fitted. Evicted.

That ain't right, says Smiler, and I'm waiting
for the pay-off when he'll scald
the bastards who betrayed him,
*that ain't right: the fox has given you a good run
and now you're killing him,* he says,
his good eye blinking.

Observing Beckett

I've watched his skin marble like a lizard's
as he sat in a bar on the Boul' Miche.
I have seen him turn his back, raise his collar
and step out towards the A3, Verney,
Dublin, the black void of the auditorium;
always his knapsack slung over his shoulder
and looking like he might be gone for good,
like the thief Augustine said was damned.

But Jim has observed him at close quarters,
scanned the craggy camouflage for symbols,
scoured the raptor features, come away unscathed.
Because Jim, too, could hold his whisky,
knew the importance of a maiden century,
was practiced in the art of runic script.

Go Figure

For instance James Dean, 24 years old
when he died, made up to look 58.
You do the maths.

Born 8 February 1931
at Seven Gables apartment house
Marion, Indiana (19th state); mother
died of cancer when James was only nine.
His problems multiplied.

Killed 30 September 1955
out on Highway 466 – now 46 –
at the junction with Highway 41.
Died in a fraction of a second.

Driving a Porsche Spyder 550
with one-three-zero on front and sides
– only 90 were ever made – 3.30
that afternoon he got a ticket
doing 65 in a 55 mph zone.
Pronounced dead at 5.59.

Seven days earlier, Alec Guinness
told Jimmy if he got in that car
he'd be found dead.
How does that add up?

He was 5'10", weighed
150 lbs., had had affairs
with countless men and women.
Three people were injured in the crash
– only one didn't make it,
only one was taken away.

Starred in three films. Just one, *East of Eden,*
released at the time he died. Nominated
for two posthumous Best Actor awards.

Dean's estate makes $5,000,000 every year.

You can work it out in the margin.

Interrogation Scenes

Scanned

The man at airport security
looks up and calls me forward.

I step through the metal detector
and something sets off the beeper,

something I'd forgotten I had
deep in the folds of my clothes.

And you in your cosy conning tower,
– views of fenland and sea –

you beckoned me on, x-rayed me,
cooing in your white whiskers

the day you caught me red-handed,
a packet of poems about my person.

'*Chittering' is good,* you said, and
I prefer 'rowanberries', for the rhythm.

I stretch out my arms and the man
runs the scanner over me.

This time I fob him off with a phone.

The Safe Side

It's Apollinaire's birthday, a humid day
likely to be temperamental:
morose, unpredictable,
inclined to thunder.

It's a day for the red Florentine umbrella –
to be on the safe side.

A day to steer clear of white spaces
for fear of disorientation and fever.
A day to keep hold of the silver handle,
contemplate the pattern inside the canopy,
designed to please the eye
when sheltering.

Nonetheless I step inside the gallery,
find myself standing before continents
with their depths and their heights,
their ageless insignia
like the banners of armies.

Inside or out I am anchored and blinkered,
studying symbols as the rain falls.
This is not a day to make a dash for it.

It's a day to keep a firm grip,
a day to raise your free palm,
instinctively, heavenwards.

Rescued

All I remember is that he grabbed his shoes,
his broken pumps – only those – and dived
into the water with its rime of fresh snow
feathering the surface as he struggled
to bring them ashore: half a dozen fishers
thrown into the lake by their shattered boat.

The child on the jetty clutched a plastic fairy
in a purple tutu, while her eyes traced
the grim trigonometry between the faces
of the adults.
                    His smile, when it came,
stretched beyond the arc of his teeth,
metal glinting in the dark recess,
making her think of a bright star far off in the sky.

Volcano

for Alex Hoare

A dish. A crater. A viscous lens.
A slip of piddled oil, still, watchful.

A vessel, cracked, nerve-wracked,
its veined surface slick with tricky nets

of mucous. A portent. A hiatus.
A bubbling slew, bloodshot,

about to spew liquid fire, raw,
from its glaucous tight-lipped rim,

its coated maw to heave an eclipse
of cloud into the spare blue

where nothing waits
and everything attends.

Another Place

The dust cloud has grounded my flight
so it's down to the ferry terminal
for the overnighter to Birkenhead
among truckers, bikers and all-night boozers;
music and neon keep us up till first light
and I'm wishing I'd stayed in Belfast.

After breakfast I go on deck, peer
through the mist, searching the foreshore
for those standing metal figures,
and what comes to mind are spears
of asparagus sprouting in sand dunes.

Trousers rolled up to their knees,
you can almost hear the night soil men
muttering, as they gaze out to sea,
how volcanic ash would do just as well.

Dust in the Sunlight

In the map room everyone knows their place.
Here it is quiet as a sepulchre
so that we communicate in small signs
and soundless gestures, dust in the sunlight.

We draw the lines of latitude, scan
contours for significance and observe
the passage of prevailing winds, currents
and ice floes, measure avalanches,
and the volcanoes of the deep. Even
the grids of landlocked cities have meaning,
their catchment areas, travel-to-work zones.

We know the lie of the land, its shifting
boundaries are an open secret to us.
We do not care for fixity or permanence,
we watch for movement, calculate bearings,
plot the course to the last degree.

This is ancient and modern, starscapes
and lasers, dust in the sunlight.
Quiet as a sepulchre.
                                        The sheer walls
of the map room rise like cliffs, a clerestory
illuminates the smallest of symbols.
But no door or spy-hole breaks the plane
and there is no key save our imagining.

Moving Image

This is the image he holds in his mind,
  the tide of sleep tugging it back and forth:
    a deserted station, he stares down the track,
the train a speck where the rails converge.

He spins with vertigo unable to tell
  if the train is stationary, advancing
    or moving away; feels the same about
the time, even the air he breathes.

He recalls a journey by bus, the road straight,
  stretching on for miles, vanishing point
    liquefying in the heat. He had turned
to the window, peered through his dull reflection

at distant mountains barely in motion.
  In the foreground the desert's edge sped by.
    He could taste the dust. In the shadow
of a tree an old man knelt to some deathly act.

He remembers thinking there would come a time
  when this moment would haunt his memory,
    when the bus would stop by the roadside,
the man look up, the train emerge from the heat.

Interrogation Scenes

1

They play hard-cop-soft-cop inside your head,
wield the hose, dangle a bed and sleep – if only

you'll co-operate. A ceiling fan flickers,
you fear a fit, can't shake the voices

of the other diners and the ageing lovers
at the corner table who coo to one another,

touch fingertips, make goo-goo eyes. "Get wise.
Make it easy. Confess – you know you want to."

The cops are getting twitchy. You hide
the book of poems, order chicken cacciatore.

2

There was that time they quizzed you
on the meaning of repentance, a crowd

of biblebashers somewhere in the mid-West.
Speaking in tongues, you had them spellbound,

they ate out of your hand when you quoted
the parable of God-and-the-circus-tent,

began to think you might get away with it
might even have a talent for the pastoral bit,

as long as your libido didn't let you down –
as long as you avoided thunderbolts.

3

You try telling the old familiar tales:
the car smash, the rope burns,

that incident with the cereal bowl.
They listen with feigned concern.

You use the same words: "sobbing wreck",
"died in my arms", "down to the bone".

They wonder how you remain so calm,
but they have ways of getting blood from stones.

If only they knew the half of it:
how you long to blab about *love-in-a-mist.*

4

In Babylon they massage your scalp,
anoint you with oils, soap

the thin strands splayed like deltas
across your forehead. In the dark you feel

your bulk collapse into bundled straw,
you see a shadow eclipse the low

moon's face like a bloodstain. You rise
with a vague memory of bruises

and the taste of salt on your tongue,
wondering if they have yet begun.

The Security of Regulation

Found poem, relic of the Pol Pot regime, Cambodia

You must answer accordingly to my questions.
Don't turn them away.

Don't try to hide the facts
by making pretexts this and that.
You are strictly prohibited to contest me.

Don't be a fool for you are a chap who dare
to thwart the revolution.

You must immediately answer my questions
without wasting time to reflect.

Don't tell me either about your immoralities
or the essence of the revolution.

While getting lashes or electrification
you must not cry at all.

Do nothing, sit still and wait for my orders.
If there is no order, keep quiet.

When I ask you to do something
you must do it right away without protesting.

Don't make pretext about Kampuchea Kromin
in order to hide your secret or traitor.

If you don't follow all the above rules
you shall get many lashes of electric wire.

If you disobey any point of my regulations
you shall get either ten lashes
or five shocks of electric discharge.

While getting lashes or electrification
you must not cry at all.

If there is no order, keep quiet.

Worlds Apart

I dig a round hole
and plant a tree.

You dig a square hole
and bury a child.

I fill my hole with scoops of loam,
tamp it with my heel
and water the soil.

You fill your hole with coffin wood,
handfuls of red clay
and mother's tears.

My tree bursts into life.
Your child lies still.

I watch the cut worm flail
before it heals.

You've never seen a worm
and have no word for healing.

Pretty as a Picture

If you saw it from the air, their first garden,
you might think: picture postcard.

You might make out marrow plants,
though not their rough stems, coarseness
of the leaves shading the blooms. You'd hardly notice
scarlet runners on their rods, black-eyed-Susan
climbing the wall.
                              In the shed the rack of tools –
inherited, borrowed – would be hidden from view,
and the smooth roofslates of the house itself
would obscure the kitchen's sanded floors,
walls in *buttermilk* and *sunflower*, upstairs
the unmade bed beneath a low ceiling.

You would not hear whispers from the bedroom,
a slap, the stifled cry that follows,
tears draining into the sheet, into the night.

Though you might observe the door to the street,
still ajar, still trembling.

Trace Memory

He leaves a trail of clues along the way,
the obvious ones between the pages

of books: ticket stubs from concerts and plays
or journeys he's made; messages

from friends written on tasteful postcards,
photographs, cuttings from the papers –

anything that makes a decent bookmark,
a memory to be savoured later.

And what of all the rest: things he'll say
the keys, the clothes, the things he sheds;

fingerprints or strands of hair, DNA,
layers of dust and skin beneath the bed?

These, the trace elements of his story,
are all that he's prepared to let them know

and still retain some air of mystery –
like a teaser for a sleazy peepshow.

Easing the Aching

Whatever the combination of x and y,
whether we're descended from apes or fish

or specks of stardust from some distant sky,
it all comes down to worms and ash

unless in this long wind-shadow we leave a trace
of something more than is unveiled

by powdered brush or u/v rays:
a gold torc surfacing in a ploughed field,

the note that startles in a yellow margin,
a tower of learning and the sea beyond,

more joy than you or I imagine
in the comfort of remembered song.